THE
BIBLE
YEAR

*A Journey Through Scripture
in 365 Days*

MAGREY R. DEVEGA

Abingdon Press | Nashville

THE BIBLE YEAR
A Journey Through Scripture in 365 Days
Pastor Guide

978-1-7910-2345-4

21 22 23 24 25 26 27 28 29 30 — 10 9 8 7 6 5 4 3 2 1
MANUFACTURED IN THE UNITED STATES OF AMERICA

⚡ AMPLIFY MEDIA

Enrich your small group experience with weekly videos for *The Bible Year,* available through Amplify Media.

Amplify Media is a multi-media platform that delivers high quality, searchable content with an emphasis on Wesleyan perspectives for church-wide, group, or individual use on any device at any time. In a world of sometimes overwhelming choices, Amplify gives church leaders media capabilities that are contemporary, relevant, effective and, most importantly, affordable and sustainable.

With Amplify Media you can:

- Provide a reliable source of Christian content through a Wesleyan lens for teaching, training, and inspiration in a customizable library,
- Deliver your own preaching and worship content in a way your congregation knows and appreciates,
- Build your church's capacity to innovate with engaging content and accessible technology,
- Equip your congregation to better understand the Bible and its application, and
- Deepen discipleship beyond the church walls.

Sign up for Amplify Media at:
https://www.amplifymedia.com/annual-pricing.
Use *Promo Code BibleYear22* at checkout.*

To Kathy Farmer, Tom Boomershine,
Tom Dozeman, and A.K.M. Adam,
for instilling in me a love for reading
and studying the Bible;

To the faithful disciples of
Hyde Park United Methodist Church
who make God's love real every day;

To Grace and Madelyn

Contents

Contents

CHAPTER 1

Reading the Whole Bible Together
Overcoming Fear and Frustration

CONNECTION

The Bible Year emerged from a year-long commitment in a single congregation to read the whole Bible together in a year. In 2017, the church I serve, Hyde Park United Methodist in Tampa, Florida, began a long-term, strategic planning process. We surveyed the congregation, spoke to people in the community, and most of all, listened to the Holy Spirit as we discerned together God's future for the church.

What emerged was a clear sense that God was calling us to deepen our discipleship, widen our reach to people around us, and unite together in common purpose, while using adaptive and creative means to do so.

One of the clearest areas for growth was in *connection*. People wanted to be more connected to God and to each other, and specifically grow deeper in their understanding of the Bible. Our church had had a long history of faithful small group ministries. Hundreds of people had taken *Disciple Bible Study*, *Covenant Bible Study*, and other long-term studies over the past thirty years. Dozens of new short-term small groups were offered each year. But still, a large percentage of our congregation still felt largely unfamiliar with

9

the Bible, despite our weekly encouragement to read it, study it together, and apply it.

It is not that people did not want to. Quite the opposite. Our congregational surveys suggested that people were identifying their desire for deeper connection to God and each other with a desire to read and understand the Bible.

So, when our vision plan was adopted in 2018, one of the first actions we took was to look for some way to bridge that gap, some way to link a reading of the Bible with a deepened sense of connection among the congregation.

And the idea for reading the whole Bible together was born.

We called it The Bible Project 2020. Our staff and lay team spent all of 2019 developing the unique resources and leadership infrastructure that would allow us to undertake the most ambitious biblical journey many of us had ever taken.

We would read the Bible, cover to cover, from January to December.

We slated 2020 as our year of reading the Bible together. We would cast the vision to the whole congregation and encourage every person to be involved through individual reading, small group participation, and weekly worship. We would make the case for why reading the Bible as a congregation in a year would be a powerful, transformative experience and help them develop daily practices that they would carry with them for the rest of their lives. I'll share with you how we cast the vision for this project in the next chapter.

We would develop an array of resources to help strengthen people along the way, including a weekly podcast featuring biblical scholars from around the country, a daily devotional, an online study group, and, most importantly, weekly small groups. We would align all our discipleship ministries for all ages to go through the Bible together, including our children and youth who would follow their own separate but parallel track. I'll share with you all the resources at your disposal that are part of *The Bible Year* in chapter 3.

Then there was weekly worship. Our clergy would preach through the Bible, all fifty-two weeks, while still observing the liturgical seasons and high holy days. I'll share with you how we structured the readings to coincide with those seasons in chapter 4, along with other options you might consider.

All along the way, we would dive into the toughest questions that people would ask about the Bible, not ignoring the tough readings, but addressing them with curiosity and faithfulness. I'll share with you in chapter 5 how you might help your congregation think through the dry and unsettling parts of the Bible.

A PROFOUND IMPACT

We began the journey on January 1, 2020, not knowing how our world would be turned upside down by a global pandemic. But God had an amazing sense of timing. As our church campuses shut down and our worship services and programs shifted to a whole new virtual world of digital platforms, we all sensed the prospect of growing increasingly isolated and disconnected from each other, and from our normal rhythms and routines.

Instead, reading the Bible together had the opposite effect. It was a unifying force over the arc of the whole unsettling year. The weekly small groups became a lifeline of connection for people of all ages, who often looked forward to their video calls as a reliable source for camaraderie and companionship.

Most remarkable of all, we found time and again that the biblical passages we were studying at the time came to us at just the right moment.

+ Our displacement from the worship spaces of the church cast new light on our readings of the Babylonian Exile;
+ The divisions between the Northern and Southern Kingdoms gave us new understanding in the political and ideological divisions afflicting our country;

- The prophetic texts gave us timely words to speak with humility and justice into the racial reckoning we were going through as a country;
- And as we entered the fall of 2020 acknowledging the hurt, suffering, and brokenness of our world, the Gospel readings began on Labor Day weekend, and the familiar stories of Jesus gave us new and deeper insights into the power and love of God.

When December 31, 2020, arrived, people were effusive in describing the impact the journey had on them.

If you had asked me years ago about the prospects of this church reading the Bible cover to cover together in a year, and aligning our ministries around making that happen, I would have responded with great skepticism. Too much fear. Too much frustration. Too much that could go wrong. But now, I can't imagine having gone through 2020 in any other way. It helped us not only survive, but thrive, during a global pandemic.

And it can be the same for your congregation, whatever you may experience in the year ahead. It can help you grow closer to God, to one another other, and to the power of the Bible.

FEAR AND FRUSTRATION

Let's admit up front that the idea of leading a congregation in a yearlong reading of the Bible, cover to cover, is daunting, if not downright scary. We can more readily come up with reasons *not* to do it, rather than reasons for it. All those reasons are understandable, many of which we will address in the upcoming pages.

It's not that we don't believe in the power of the Bible, or in the importance of reading it, applying it, and living it. After all, you would likely not be in the position you're in, let alone picking up this book, if you did not hold those convictions in some way. We preach and teach from the Bible, encourage people to be in a small group to study it, and call people to spend time in it every day. We turn to it for words of comfort, draw courage from it to proclaim words of justice, and ground our congregations in its authority.

But actually *read* it? Cover to cover? As a whole congregation?

There are reasons few congregations ever attempt to do this together. What if the congregation doesn't want to do it? What if everyone loses interest partway through? What if we as preachers and lay leaders grow weary of it? And then there are the really deep questions. What if, after reading through the Bible, people have a *worse* opinion of the Bible? Or worse still: What if people have their faith shaken, instead of strengthened?

I would summarize all those reasons with two words: *fear* and *frustration*.

The fear comes from the parts of the Bible that we think we understand, which suggests ideas about God and the faith that are hard to believe. What do we do with the images of God that are unsettling? Or the violence that people commit in the name of God? Or the prospect of losing our faith when we cannot reconcile these stories with our modern experience?

The frustration comes from the parts of the Bible that we do not understand, and therefore find it hard to believe or appreciate. What do we do with the parts of the Bible that seem antiquated and archaic? Or that just don't make any sense to us when we read them? What do we do with the strange-sounding laws and the obscure prophetic oracles? What do we do with the hard-to-pronounce names and places? What do we do with the seemingly endless pages of dry references, censuses and genealogies, and detailed instructions that will feel like walking through a wilderness? Again, do we risk the prospect of losing our faith when we cannot reconcile these strange stories with our modern ears?

It is not that we don't believe in the power of the Bible, or the reasons for reading it. But fear and frustration are major factors that would lead us to pick and choose what we read, at our own pace, leaving aside the hard questions we feel like we alone are asking.

So, with those two significant barriers in mind, why spend a whole year reading the Bible in its entirety? How can *The Bible Year* show us how to overcome those fears and alleviate those frustrations?

1. *The Bible Year* encourages us to read the Bible *together.*

I know people who have tried to read the Bible cover to cover on their own, and it often elicits far more questions about their own faith than if they were to read the Bible in conversation with others. Reading these texts as a congregation, especially in the context of small groups, can allow for a safe, supportive forum to pose the kinds of questions that people would otherwise wrestle with on their own. Often, it is the mere freedom and permission to ask these questions aloud of others that can itself encourage people who would otherwise struggle with the faith. Most importantly, reading the Bible together can elicit novel insights from the diversity of voices around the room, unlocking new, life-giving ways to look at a text.

2. *The Bible Year* encourages us to read the Bible in its *entirety.*

Imagine reading a novel by skipping around randomly from page to page, out of order. Imagine reading a textbook in which you begin in the middle, without reading the basic concepts at the beginning. Imagine trying to fully understand a book by relying only on the quotes that others tell you. The Bible is best read in its entirety, from a literary and theological perspective. Understanding the grand narrative of God's self-revealing, self-giving love for humanity is the critical connective tissue that allows us to not get too bogged down on the fearsome, frustrating parts of the Bible.

3. *The Bible Year* reminds us to take the Bible *seriously,* without having to take all of it literally.

My favorite metaphor to explain this concept comes from my friend and clergy colleague Jim Harnish, who thinks about the Bible in terms of the Sunday newspaper. When we thumb through the different sections and pages of the Sunday paper, we know that we are to read its various sections differently. We read the front-page headlines differently from the way we read the editorials and op-ed section. One we view through the lens of verifiable historical record, the other we view as persuasion pieces. We read the movie reviews differently from the sports box scores, differently from the obituaries, differently from the comics and classified ads.

Reading through the Bible together shows us the breadth and diversity of its literary genres. Along the way, we can ask critical questions about how to understand the Torah differently from the way we understand Kings and Chronicles, which are different still from the Wisdom Literature, the prophets, the Gospels, the Epistles, and the apocalyptic literature of Daniel and Revelation.

The resources of *The Bible Year* contain a robust collection of insights from biblical preachers and experts from around the country. You will want to include the weekly videos as part of your congregation's journey. The podcasts developed by our church are also available from Hyde Park UMC, titled "The Bible Project 2020," and feature reflections on the weekly texts from a variety of biblical scholars.

4. *The Bible Year* helps us read the Bible *hopefully*.

As a preacher, you will have numerous opportunities throughout the year to address the potentially troublesome parts of the Bible in your sermons and other weekly reflections. It may be the most concentrated and direct chance you will have to answer these hard questions with answers that are both helpful and hopeful.

In chapter 5, I offer a few different ways that you might think about the dry and disconcerting parts of Scripture, particularly the Torah and the Prophets, and the images of violence throughout the Old Testament. You can offer the congregation different ways to see those texts that elicit gratitude and hope, rather than fear and frustration.

5. *The Bible Year* helps us read the Bible *regularly*.

Most importantly, reading the Bible every day can help people in your congregation develop the spiritual "muscle memory" to make daily devotions a regular part of their life, even after *The Bible Year* concludes. Many of the small groups in our church that read through the Bible together decided to continue meeting into the following year. People could reread texts in the future that used to give them difficulty, seeing them with fresh understanding and new applications.

And the impact goes beyond the discipline of just Scripture reading. People in our congregation discovered passions and interests in themselves that led to service in and through our faith community. Having seen the benefit of solidarity and spiritual companionship, they became more generous in their financial giving, recognizing how their generosity contributes to transformative life change. And the reach of *The Bible Year* extended far beyond the church, through our podcasts, online services, virtual small group, and most importantly, through word-of-mouth invitation to people who joined us along the way.

The Bible Year is a powerful, meaningful journey through the greatest book of all time. Reading it together will help people in your congregation overcome their fear and frustration and will transform their lives.

Welcome to the journey!

CHAPTER 2

The Power of Story
Casting the Vision to the Congregation

It's one thing to be convinced yourself that reading the entire Bible as a congregation is a good idea. It is quite another to cast that vision and claim a compelling argument why people should do it. And it may be a hard sell to key leaders, asking them to devote time and energy to helping make it happen.

That was certainly the case for our congregation. Even though we could draw a straight-line connection between our vision plan and the reasons for this project, people still needed to be convinced. It began with our staff, many of whom were reluctant to change their effective, long-established routines. It extended to key leaders who were justifiably skeptical. It took the first few months of 2019 to get the whole congregation to buy into the idea before we could spend the rest of the year developing the resources and systems needed to make it work.

Regardless of whether your congregation has paid staff or key volunteers, churches of any size and context will be transformed by reading the Bible together. But you will need to begin by lifting up for them the vision for *The Bible Year*, helping them to understand the journey ahead and to be inspired by the potential outcomes of doing this together.

17

The goal of this chapter is to give you some guidance on how to talk to your key leaders, and it is drawn directly out of presentations I made to various leadership teams at Hyde Park UMC, so that by the fall of 2019, people became excited to begin the journey. You likely will not have a full year to prepare your congregation, so these tips will be beneficial to you as you lead your people swiftly to accept the challenge.

ACKNOWLEDGE THE BARRIERS

Just as this book began with naming fear and frustration as the primary obstacles to regular Bible reading, it would be important to acknowledge these realities as you cast the vision to your congregation. At the beginning of each conversation with key leaders in the church, I said I understood the reasons people might be skeptical to do this project. We hear them regularly:

+ There's not enough time. We are busy people, and there is a lot more to do than we have hours in a day.
+ There's lots of confusion: the words and names and places are too hard to pronounce and impossible to understand.
+ And here's a really big one: there are parts of the Bible that are troubling. All the violence, and destruction, and anger— some of it commanded and even committed by God.

You will likely have other reasons to add to the list, all of which are significant. You can acknowledge them up front. Underlying each of them is a larger cultural issue. We are decades removed from the era when biblical literacy was more commonplace in our culture and more people grew up with at least some basic understanding of the stories of the Bible. But those days are long gone, for better and for worse. We can't assume that a person had the importance of Bible reading instilled in them at an early age.

So, given those barriers, what is the *why?* What is at the heart of a vision to read the Bible every day?

For me, the key to casting a vision for this journey is the word *story*.

FOCUS ON THE STORY

You may not have ever thought of it this way, but we see reality in terms of stories. Stories of triumph and loss, good versus evil, adversity versus perseverance. Our brains, perhaps now more than ever, look at the world in story terms. And that includes your life and mine.

Whether we realize it or not, we see ourselves as the chief characters of our own stories. *And you and I want to live our stories better.* We are trying to be a good parent to our children. We are trying to overcome obstacles to not only survive, but thrive. We wonder what the next chapter, or even the next page, of our lives will bring. We need to find the best way to live the best story that we believe God has called us to live.

The Bible Year is built on the premise that there is no better way for you to learn to live your story as God intends it than for you to find yourself in the Bible's stories. Did you know there are more than six hundred stories in this book? And each one is an invitation for you to learn how to live your own story.

+ Are you fearful? There are stories here for you.
+ Are you worried about your health? There are stories here for you.
+ Do you want to be the best parent or sibling or family member you can be? There are stories here for you.
+ Do you wonder where God is in the midst of suffering? Find your story in here.
+ Are you confused about your future? Find your story in here. In fact, I remember when I was in college, I read and reread the story of Joseph in Genesis and it gave me encouragement to make it through a tough time in early adulthood.

My bishop in the Florida Conference, Ken Carter, is fond of using this personal analogy. He has admitted publicly that he has never read a Harry Potter book. Making that admission generally elicits some reaction of disbelief from many in whatever audience he is addressing. He says that it is not because he dislikes the books; he has just chosen for whatever reason to not read these particular books.

He understands that there is a whole subculture built around an adoration of the series. Whole segments of the population have found camaraderie in each other, located themselves in the story, and find within it applicable meaning for their lives. They have made journeys to their "holy" places: theme parks built around the wizarding world, where people can immerse themselves as first-person pilgrims in this corporate journey. And he understands why people feel compelled to "proselytize" him toward becoming as avid a fan of the books as they are.

The metaphor he is building, of course, connects with the ambivalence people might feel when it comes to the Bible. Yes, there are legions of people in the church devoted to the creative power of the Bible. There are people who have spent their whole lives reading it, studying it, extracting nuances from it, and finding their identity in it. And there are others who vehemently work against it, believing it to be a collection of texts that have on the whole done more harm than good. They oppose it or ridicule it.

But to many people, their view of the Bible is not derision or condescension on the one hand, or passionate immersion and advocacy on the other. It is ambivalence. They're not sure how they feel about it, or how they will feel once they begin reading in earnest. Is it worth the time and effort it will take to read and understand? And the desire they may have to "get into" the Bible may be overridden by a sense that everyone else has everything figured out when it comes to these texts. So why bother?

Acknowledge first and foremost—and repeatedly—that the fact that people come into this journey with differing starting points is actually a strength. There is no common baseline of understanding or exposure when it comes to the Bible. And by the end of the journey, everyone will be able to come away with this central, personal conviction:

I see God in this story. I see myself in this story. I see us in this story.

This premise is what sets this journey apart from a mere book club, in which people find meaning in stories outside the Bible. Other books like novels, biographies, and collections of poetry may contain profound meaning, and might even be easier to read. But the Bible is central to our faith, drawing us together into a story that connects us to our earliest spiritual ancestors. As people of faith, we become characters in the Bible, walking alongside them as they discovered truths about God and the human experience. No other book, from a faith perspective, has that power.

The key to reading the Bible without fear or frustration is to see that ultimately, this is a story about God, about our relationship with God, and about our relationship with one another. Yes, biblical texts often contain strange words and imagery. But beneath it all, the Bible is a record of how our spiritual ancestors wrestled over how to understand the nature and character of God and humanity. Reading the Bible means that their story can become our story. Their struggles, revelations, and resolutions permit us to ponder the same questions that are at the heart of these texts:

Where do I see God in this story? What does this passage show me about God's relentless desire to restore a broken world? What does it tell me about God's love, justice, and righteousness? What surprising depictions of God's character challenge my assumptions and stretch me to think about God in a different way?

Where do I see myself in this story? What are human beings doing in this story that I find troublesome or commendable? What would I do if I were in this story? How does this passage reveal aspects of my life that I would rather ignore? What does this text teach me about faithfulness to God?

Where do I see us in this story? What does this passage teach me about human relationships? How can this text show us how to be in community with each other? What does this passage reveal about sins and injustices in our culture today? How does this story remind me that being a part of community is better than following God by myself?

When we read the Bible with questions like these in mind, we find ourselves among its pages, wrestling over the very questions that the people of God did generations ago.

So, *The Bible Year* is not about creating biblical experts. Overcoming fear and frustration does not suggest that people will walk away with zero doubts and perfect clarity about the Bible. And it is certainly not intended to form people who can argue and defend their biblical perspectives and interpretations.

As you cast the vision for *The Bible Year* in your congregation, remember to focus on the story. This journey is about creating a welcoming, nurturing environment in which people are connected to each other, stay on track with the readings together, and ultimately discover a deeper purpose and meaning in the stories of the Bible.

You cannot state the premise enough: People will be impacted by this journey in positive ways. Everyone who goes on this journey will be changed in some way. People will feel connected to God and connected to each other, because they have read these stories together.

And after 365 days of doing this, people will develop new muscle memory to be able to have a quiet time with God every day for the rest of their lives. They will discover new stories that will become their new favorites because they see themselves in the pages. They will discover new friendships in a group. They will see familiar stories in new ways because they will learn from each other.

They will learn to read the Bible without fear and frustration.

And the Spirit will work more times than you will be able to count. When someone says, I read a passage this week that was exactly what I needed to read because of what was happening in my life or in the world—that will be God working, and it will happen over and over and over again.

CHAPTER 3

Resources for the Journey
Impactful and Flexible

Since any journey requires preparation and resources, *The Bible Year* includes a number of materials to guide your congregation. They are primarily designed to encourage people to keep up with the daily readings and to maintain their connection to one another. They also provide insights into the readings that will enable them to approach the texts without fear or frustration.

The important thing to keep in mind is that all of this material is flexible and adaptable to your context and timing. There may be valid reasons why your congregation cannot or will not spend twelve consecutive months doing this journey. Your congregation may wish to begin the journey and take a break for a season or two. You may wish to take these resources and customize them for your congregation, or to spend a shorter period of time on a focused section of Scripture, such as the Gospels or the Prophets.

While there are great benefits to reading the Bible together in a twelve-month period, it is important to start somewhere, and guide your congregation to begin building the muscle memory to make daily Bible reading a vital spiritual practice.

THE READING PLAN

The reading plan comes from the one used in the *NRSV Daily Bible* (HarperCollins). It is an excellent resource, but that version or translation is not required to go on this journey. You may encourage your congregation to use any translation. I find the CEB and NIV especially helpful, as well as the NRSV. The readings for the most part are relatively short, around three to five chapters per day.

The plan we used at Hyde Park in 2020 is found in the appendix of this pastor guide, and it includes not only the daily readings but also the weekly preaching texts, the sermon series titles, and the seasons of the liturgical year. The next chapter will go into further detail over how the daily readings match up with the major seasons of the liturgical year.

WEEKLY WORSHIP

Worship is an important part of this journey, as it provides a corporate element to experiencing the stories together. The daily readings will illuminate the texts shared in worship, which will in turn shape the reading of the daily texts. Even though this journey takes place over fifty-two weeks, it can be broken down into smaller, consecutive worship series based on sections of the Bible and the liturgical seasons. This will be explored in further detail in the next chapter.

Preaching through the Bible will help worshippers see connections among the stories and grasp how they fit together in the grand narrative arc of the Bible. As a preacher, you will have the opportunity to not only share your understanding of the texts, but insights into how these stories can shape the faith and life of the congregation. Weekly worship offers a critical corporate element to the journey.

DAILY DEVOTIONAL

The Bible Year features a daily devotional that can be used as a companion reader to the daily Scriptures. Each day focuses on a particular text, or some overall aspect of the readings, that will guide the individual in their own spiritual reading. The devotions are short and often include practical questions that invite the reader to reflect on and apply the readings to his or her own life. By the end of the year, this devotional becomes a kind of journal to record a person's questions, conclusions, and applications.

Each week also begins with an introduction from me, as I share a longer reflection on some aspect of the reading. You might find these reflections helpful in shaping your own preaching and writing to the congregation, and they could be an added conversation topic for small group study.

WEEKLY VIDEOS

The material includes insightful teaching from a team of gifted preachers and writers, who each week appear in a brief video that is available on the online Amplify platform (www.amplifymedia.com). These videos offer scholarly and pastoral wisdom into each week's readings, and can be a central component to your small groups' experience. They can also be used by individuals in order to enhance their daily reading, as well as in worship to supplement your sermon or worship experience.

SMALL GROUPS

The small group experience is a central component to *The Bible Year*. As formative as it will be for people to read the daily Scriptures on their own, participation in a small group will offer greater spiritual transformation. In these small groups, persons will be able to share their insights and questions with each other, in a community of mutual respect and care. Together, they will locate their shared experience as a group in the wider narratives of the Bible and discover the power of reading, studying, and praying together. Most importantly, they will develop the "muscle memory" of being in a small group long-term and may even continue meeting after the journey is over.

Often, it is in the context of being in a small group like this that people begin to see their commitment to Christ deepen and their spirituality mature. As a result, it is even likely that people will emerge from these groups eager to serve more faithfully out of their giftedness, and step into opportunities for service and leadership in and through the church.

OTHER RESOURCES

There are several other possible resources that you may choose to develop to customize and enhance your congregation's journey:

1. Children and Youth Resources

Our church decided early in the development of this project that we did not want it to be geared only for adults in the congregation. For it to have lasting, maximum value, we encouraged families to do it together, including the youth and children.

Naturally, expecting children to read through the same daily reading plan over a year's time was not advisable, especially due to some of the content that would be confusing or even troubling to them. Youth had the option of doing the same daily readings as the adults.

But overall, our children and youth teams created plans for their weekly lessons for children's Sunday school and youth group, in order to cover the major sections and stories of the Bible over a year's time. Much of their material came from pre-produced curriculum from Christian publishers, which are listed in the appendix of this pastor's guide.

Your children and youth leaders may choose to use similar curriculum, or generate new material on their own. Either way, encouraging children and youth to be part of the same journey will be an exciting addition to the year.

2. Weekly Podcast

When we first read the Bible together at Hyde Park UMC, our church opted to produce a weekly podcast, which became a centerpiece for our small groups and daily readings. We produced about sixty episodes over the year's time, each one featuring a different biblical scholar, clergy, or lay-person from around the country with particular expertise in that portion of the Bible. It was led by a team of lay members who hosted each episode and interviewed the guests. These episodes ran the course of 2020. While some of the conversations include references to events occurring at that time, the vast majority of the material is spent exploring the richness of the readings for that week.

Our weekly podcast continues to be available for free and can be accessed on the podcast site of Hyde Park UMC, called "The Bible Project 2020." That and other resources are listed in the appendix of this pastor guide.

3. Online Group

Even though we were encouraging everyone in the church to be part of a small group, highlighting the advantage of reading the Bible with others, we recognized that not everyone would choose to do so. It was important to create an opportunity for such individuals to still be in conversation with other people, albeit through a virtual, online format. So, we created a private Facebook group and invited anyone to be a part of it. It became a helpful way for me and other leaders to be in conversation with people as they offered their own insights and raised questions. Each day, a volunteer posted a short reflection and question based on the day's Scripture text, and people responded with their own comments. You might ask a volunteer to post his or her own reflection or even a short Scripture quotation from the day's text followed by a question. Even something as simple as "How is God speaking to you through this passage?" will invite conversation.

Creating such a group could be a simple and effective way to keep people engaged and connected, even if they are not part of a small group of their own.

4. Mission and Service Opportunities

Prior to the start of the pandemic, we had envisioned aligning our missions and service opportunities throughout the year to be in sync with whatever section of the Bible we would be reading. Doing so, we reasoned, would be a great way to create practical, impactful interpretations of the Bible. Though the pandemic limited our ability to do this in our own congregation in 2020, I encourage you to explore opportunities like this in your own setting as circumstances allow.

Such ideas might include:

+ Implementing an environmental clean-up day during the stories of Creation or visiting a wildlife sanctuary during the stories of Noah.

+ Camping as a family to celebrate the beauty of God's creation and the importance of family connections, as reflected in the family stories of Genesis.

+ Hosting a speaker's event with an emphasis on criminal justice and prison system reform during the time that you read about the Israelites' slavery in Egypt.

+ Raising money for the elimination of medical debt for economically disadvantaged people while reading the description of the Jewish tradition of jubilee, in which debts were forgiven and slaves were set free.

+ Hosting a book drive for a local elementary school during the time that you read the Wisdom Literature, particularly the Book of Proverbs, which espouses the value of wisdom.

+ Holding a donation drive for a local food pantry, or volunteering at a local feeding site while reading the call by the prophets to care for the poor.

+ Having a service day, in which church members go into the community to help with various projects in the spirit of the early church in Acts.

+ Hosting a speaker's panel and discussion about anti-racism, during the reading of Paul's 1 and 2 Corinthians and other Epistles that talk about breaking down divisions among people.

5. Periodic Celebrations

It will be helpful to plan some congregation-wide events throughout the year to reenergize people along the way, synchronized with corresponding celebrations in the Bible. These moments allow the whole church to celebrate what they have experienced so far, connect with one another, and anticipate the next section of the Bible ahead.

Some possibilities include:

+ An observance of the Jewish Passover seder, inviting a local rabbi to offer an instructive Passover meal during the reading of Exodus, honoring the traditions of the Jewish people and discovering the roots of our faith in the Hebrew Bible.
+ A hymn festival or songfest, corresponding to the reading of the Psalms.
+ A poetry reading or open mic series during the reading of the prophets, echoing the public performance art of the prophets.
+ An early Christmas-style celebration upon the beginning of the reading of the Gospels.
+ A global missions celebration during the reading of Acts, recognizing local and worldwide missions, agencies, and missionaries the congregation supports throughout the year.
+ A letter-writing campaign, writing notes of encouragement to people in the congregation and to local public servants while reading the letters of Paul.
+ A joy-filled closing celebration at the culmination of the journey at the end of the year.

FLEXIBILITY: CUSTOMIZING THE JOURNEY

There may be good reasons why your congregation feels that a whole year through the Bible is not a practical option for them. The Bible Year material has some flexibility, with ways for you to customize the journey so that it works best for you.

The reading plan can be broken into three blocks of readings, four months each. You might choose to spend four months reading from Genesis to Job, and take a break of a few weeks or months, followed by a second four-month block of the Psalms through the prophets. Then you can pick it up later to do the entire New Testament in a final four-month block. Moving through the Bible in this way would take your congregation longer than a year, but it would be broken up by periods that might make sense for you. For example, each block of four months might take place during three consecutive fall seasons, or three consecutive summers.

As you will see in the next chapter, your worship plan can be conceived as thirteen distinct worship series, rather than one long, fifty-two-week series. This will afford your church flexibility in how to approach the readings and break up potential feelings of monotony. It will also provide opportunities to set the plan aside for a short period to focus on a different set of Scriptures—for instance, using lectionary texts during the season of Lent—and return to the basic plan at a natural point.

WELCOMING PEOPLE THROUGHOUT THE YEAR

Naturally, it is hoped that throughout the year you will be welcoming new people into the church, people who were not necessarily with you when the program began at the start of the year. It is important to build in entry points for them to jump into the journey in a way that enables them to feel connected right away. Here are some suggestions:

Plan for the start of new small groups to begin, perhaps once a quarter, for people who will enter *The Bible Year* together.

Record your sermons and archive them for video watching or audio listening, so that people can "binge watch" any parts of the journey that they have missed. Alternatively, have printed manuscripts of your sermons available.

Designate periodic "welcome back" days to invite people who have gotten behind in their readings or decided to step away from the journey for whatever reason. Natural moments along the way include the start of liturgical seasons like Lent or Pentecost, the start of the Psalms, and the beginning of the New Testament.

CHAPTER 4

Scheduling the Year Ahead
Preaching, Worship, and Liturgical Seasons

One of the first obvious questions about spending a year of daily readings through the Bible is how such a journey might connect with the liturgical seasons and high holy days. It's one thing to begin the year by reading Genesis or spending the summer reading the Psalms or reading the Gospels in the fall. Those sections and seasons fit together rather nicely. But what about Lent and Advent? What about Ash Wednesday, Easter Sunday, Pentecost, and Christmas? How can a church observe those days credibly, while staying on track with the daily readings?

Those are among the first matters that require careful planning from the beginning. It also provided for us at Hyde Park some of the most serendipitous and timely outcomes of the whole project, which can certainly happen for your congregation.

A helpful starting point is to recognize that *The Bible Year* is not intended to be one contiguous, fifty-two-week series. Preaching through it this way is not impossible, but it is more likely to lead to stagnation and burnout along the way. Instead, we recommend you break the journey down into individual worship series, which can then coincide with the different seasons throughout the year. Each series can have its own title, thematic

33

direction, graphics, and marketing. This allows people the chance to reengage with a new section of the Bible if by chance they have drifted away from the daily readings for a period of time.

In 2020 at Hyde Park, we broke the year into the following thirteen worship series:

Series Title	Dates	Section	Season
"The Story Begins"	Jan. 1 – Feb. 1	Genesis, Exodus	Epiphany
"Road Rules"	Feb. 2 – Feb. 25	Leviticus, Deuteronomy	Epiphany
"Holy Character"	Feb. 26 – April 12	Joshua – 2 Chronicles	Lent
"A Spiritual Makeover"	April 13 – May 2	Ezra – Job	Easter
"God's Favorite Playlist"	May 3 – June 6	Psalms	Pentecost
"The Wise Life"	June 7 – July 4	Proverbs, Ecclesiastes	Pentecost
"Hope for Hard Times"	July 5 – Aug. 1	Isaiah, Jeremiah	Pentecost
"Faith When It Counts"	Aug. 2 – Aug. 29	Ezekiel – the Minor Prophets	Pentecost
"The Jesus Story"	Aug. 30 – Oct. 24	Matthew – John	Pentecost (Fall)
"Ancestry: Our Spiritual DNA"	Oct. 25 – Nov. 7	Acts	Pentecost
"Step into this Story"	Nov. 8 – Nov. 28	Romans – Colossians	Stewardship
"The Good Life"	Nov. 29 – Dec. 26	1-2 Thessalonians – Jude	Advent
"Amen, Hallelujah"	Dec. 27 – Dec. 31	Revelation	New Year

In the appendix of this pastor guide, you can find the comprehensive schedule of how we did it at Hyde Park UMC, including the Sunday Scriptures, key theme words, and daily readings.

Note: You will see in the appendix that the first week's readings contain only four days. This gives you flexibility as your congregation begins the program, since January 1 is not the same weekday from one year to the next (and some may wish to start it at a different time of the year). For instance, in 2022, January 1 is a Saturday. You might use Sunday, January 2, to introduce the whole program, invite everyone to begin reading (Day 1) on Wednesday, January 5, and begin the first sermon series on January 9.

In theory, this approach would have allowed us to have continuous on-ramps, and even off-ramps, for small groups that decide to take a break from meeting or reconvene. It was important to communicate from the beginning that if a small group needed to spend a few weeks apart, they could take a whole series off and get back together at the next one, with individuals from the small group continuing with the daily readings on their own. This was a key strategy in getting existing small groups to buy in and give it a try. It also created natural starting points for newcomers to the church to jump into a new small group at the start of a series.

In reality, what happened because of the pandemic is that most of our small groups chose to stay together for the entire year and not take any time off from gathering to discuss these texts. They shifted their meetings to online, virtual platforms during a time of social distancing. Our small groups became a lifeline for many people when they would otherwise feel isolated, and The Bible Project became the key way for our congregation to maintain connection with each other throughout the pandemic. So while we do recommend using shorter worship series as natural starting and stopping points for small groups—and being clear that groups can take a break if they feel led—don't be surprised if groups see the value in staying together continuously for the whole year.

LITURGICAL SEASONS
AND HIGH HOLY DAYS

Now we get to the question of how to coincide the daily readings with the liturgical seasons and holy days, particularly Lent and Easter, Advent and Christmas, and Pentecost. The first key determination we made was that we would still observe these seasons and days, and give them the due liturgical observance that they required. At the same time, we would allow the particular section of the Bible to illuminate for us a different way of approaching those seasons.

For Lent, we found ourselves in the Book of Judges during the week of Ash Wednesday. The timing provided an opportunity to make a rich connection between the cycle of disobedience and repentance in Judges and our ongoing need for repentance and obedience to God. Just as the Israelites fell away from following God's commandments, and God repeatedly sent judges to call them back to righteousness, Lent can be a time for us to return to faithfulness to God.

The six weeks of Lent itself were spent in the royal stories of Samuel and Kings, affording us the chance to explore the virtues and flaws of some of the Bible's most indelible figures: Saul, David, Solomon, Ahab and Jezebel, Elijah and Elisha, Josiah, and many others. From each of these major figures, we learned about how to develop character marked by faithfulness and obedience to God, from both their positive and negative examples. This was an appropriate and meaningful theme to explore during Lent, for a worship series we titled, "Holy Character."

This is not to say, of course, that I refrained from mentioning Jesus entirely in my sermons during Lent. On Palm Sunday, we included a reading from Jesus's triumphal entry into Jerusalem. On Good Friday, we returned to our church's standard remembrance of Jesus's seven last words as the day's focus. And on Easter, when we knew we would be attracting many people to worship who were not otherwise with us on the journey through the Bible, we centered on the Resurrection story from the Gospels.

Again, it was reassuring to some of our more skeptical parishioners that Lent was still going to feel "Lenten" and Easter was still going to be centered on the Resurrection. We were just going to add the valuable insights that reading through the Old Testament stories would provide us.

For Pentecost Sunday, we found ourselves in the Psalms, and while we retained a reading of Acts 2 in the service, we made easy connections to psalms of praise and jubilation, specifically Psalm 150.

The most providential alignment between the reading schedule and the calendar came at Labor Day, at the end of a long summer of reading through the prophets and reflecting on exile in the midst of a pandemic. September brought us the advent (literally) of Jesus and the Gospel readings. It was an incredible "shot in the arm" for our Bible journey, as we landed in more familiar territory with the stories of Matthew, Mark, Luke, and John. It coincided with a time of year when there is a natural renewal of energy and momentum, related to the start of the school year and the anticipation of fall activities in the church and the community.

Since our stewardship series typically happens in November, before Thanksgiving, we again turned to where we were in the Bible for guidance. Here we discovered profound insights from the Epistles, and the number of times Paul instructed, encouraged, and praised the churches for their generosity. We titled the series "Step into the Story," as a way of inviting people who have been on this yearlong journey to become more than just readers—but active participants—in the ongoing story that God is writing in and through the church. The stories of the early church, in a sense, were now our stories to continue writing.

When we arrived at Advent, we followed a similar path to that of Lent. We remained committed to observing the Sundays of Advent, while turning to where we were in the Bible to give us a different interpretive lens. It was in the Epistles of Paul that we discovered valuable teachings on how to live out the common Advent themes of peace, hope, joy, and love, in a series we titled "The Good Life." Each Sunday, we learned practical insights on how to prepare for the birth of Jesus by living the life that God intends for us. And on Christmas Eve, we focused on the birth story from Luke's Gospel, again recognizing that many people joining us that night will have been unfamiliar with our journey through the Bible up until then.

Again, the full schedule of our year is available in the appendix to this pastor's guide, and can be a model for how you might plan your year. Given the variability in how the liturgical seasons (particularly Lent) fall in any given year, you will need to be discerning and creative about how to synchronize your Bible readings with your worship calendar.

The first thing you might do is take the full reading schedule and note alongside it the major liturgical dates your church will be observing, along with the other necessary observations of your ministry year. For example, at Hyde Park we also had to accommodate our annual Youth Sunday, Confirmation Sunday, Missions Celebration Sunday, and others. Then, determine how those Sundays might be broken down into individual worship series, coinciding with the general sections of the Bible. You will discover that sometimes, the start of a series will synchronize cleanly with the start of a new book or section of the Bible. Sometimes they won't, and you can take some liberty in organizing the Sunday themes and Scriptures accordingly. In other words, there will be some Sundays when the worship Scripture will be read during the prior week, and times when it will be read afterwards. That will not disrupt your small groups too much, as they will be reading through all of the Scriptures together.

When it comes to the seasons of Lent and Advent, prayerfully discern how that section of the Bible might invite a fresh look into the standard themes of repentance and obedience (Lent) as well as preparation and expectation (Advent). You will discover that these ancient stories will take on profound new meaning as you both exegete the texts and interpret the contexts in which they will be proclaimed and lived. Our experience at Hyde Park was one of continued surprise and awe at the ways the Holy Spirit spoke to us at just the right times in just the right ways. It's my prayer that through this commitment to a year of reading the Bible together, you and your congregation will experience the same thing.

CHAPTER 5

Dry, Violent, and Unsettling
Working through the
Hard Parts of the Bible

There are a few daunting questions that people are bound to ask when it comes to reading through the entire Bible. These are based on widely held assumptions and experiences that people have regarding the Bible, and they pose challenges to convincing people to be on this journey together.

These concerns might be summarized by three broad categories of questions:

+ What do we do when we get to the dry parts of the Bible?
+ What do we do when we get to the violent parts of the Bible?
+ What do we do when we get to the unsettling depictions of God?

This chapter offers some insights that might help you guide the congregation through the dry, disillusioning, and unsettling parts of the Bible. In order to be able to get to a point where your congregation can read and understand the Bible without fear or frustration, they will need resolution to these important questions.

THE DRY PARTS:
THE LAW AND PROPHETS

What do we do when go through the really dry, repetitive, and seemingly mind-numbing parts of the Bible? Almost immediately, in just the
second month of the journey, the daily biblical readings take you through
Leviticus, Numbers, and Deuteronomy. This section of Hebrew law can be
challenging to read and understand, and is a common off-ramp for people
who would choose to leave the readings. In July and August (assuming you
begin in January), another major section of readings are potentially difficult,
when the readings go through the Major and Minor Prophets.

First, the laws. The most recurring question many people ask during
this section will likely be, "Why is there so much mind-numbing detail to
these laws?"

As an example, here is a random sample from Leviticus. This is from
22:21-25 (CEB):

> *Whenever someone presents a communal sacrifice of well-being to*
> *the* Lord *from the herd or flock—whether it is payment for a sol-*
> *emn promise or a spontaneous gift—it must be flawless to be accept-*
> *able; it must not have any imperfection. You must not present to the*
> Lord *anything that is blind or that has an injury, mutilation, warts,*
> *a rash, or scabs. You must not put any such animal on the altar as*
> *a food gift for the* Lord. *You can, however, offer an ox or sheep*
> *that is deformed or stunted as a spontaneous gift, but it will not be*
> *acceptable as payment for a solemn promise. You must not offer to*
> *the* Lord *anything with bruised, crushed, torn, or cut-off testicles.*
> *You must not do that in your land. You are not allowed to offer*
> *such animals as your God's food even if they come from a foreigner.*
> *Because these animals have blemishes and imperfections in them,*
> *they will not be acceptable on your behalf.*

Now, is there anything that seems particularly engaging, invigorating,
or life-transforming about this reading? Most people would probably say
there isn't. But is it possible that this passage will generate discussion? Are

there reasons for people to be inquisitive? Is there anything in this text that is provocative for people to ask questions?

Absolutely. In fact, it is important to create an environment throughout this journey where such questions and discussions are not only permitted but encouraged. This is why the small group experience is such a central part to *The Bible Year*. And your sermons and teachings can model the kinds of healthy questions that passages like these prompt us to ask.

What would it be like if, instead of feeling stuck through the slog of these dry parts of the Bible, we conceived of them as fertile soil to nurture critically important questions about the nature of faith and obedience?

Imagine the new insights that could be gleaned if your parishioners developed the skills to ask *these* kinds of questions:

+ Why do you think these laws were important to the Israelite people? What did this teach them about obedience to God and respect for each other?

+ What connections can we make between these laws and how the New Testament understands Jesus?

+ What laws seem irrelevant to us today, and what laws might seem valuable to us?

The bottom line is that some will find an insight in some passages, and others may not. It may be even be that most people decide that a particular passage is not worth discussing. But there is a potential in each passage of Scripture to reveal and affirm one of the key, overarching messages that run through the entire Bible:

God wants to be in a relationship with us. And God wants us to be in rela-tionship with each other.

You will want to reinforce this message all throughout the journey. God wants to be known. God does not wish to be absent or distant from us, and God does not want us to treat each other with disrespect. So, God contin-ually gives humanity pathways to be in connection with God and others.

And the pathways are always specific to that time, and that culture, and that worldview. The ways God asked the ancient Hebrews to be in connection with God and others will seem very different from our outlook today, but we can look at it objectively and appreciate how God always graciously gives human beings a way to be in a relationship with God and others.

Second, there is the section on the Prophets. Isaiah through Malachi, which will take place during July and August, will seem as dry as the summer season in which they will be read. There will be names of nations and people and kings that will seem unpronounceable and irrelevant. Passages like these do not have to be mysteries to be solved.

It may be that in these moments, the best way to help your congregation work through these texts and read them without fear or frustration is to continually reinforce a posture of humility, curiosity, and gratitude before God. Consider offering a statement like this throughout the journey:

> We may not fully understand what this passage means, and we don't have to. But we can appreciate how our spiritual ancestors found this meaningful. If God were calling you to this kind of obedience and concern for social issues, what words might God be using instead?

The overall theme during these dry parts, again, can be that God wants to be known, wants to be in a relationship with us, and wants us to be in a relationship with others. That's what the word *covenant* points to, after all—a deep, committed relationship to God and to others—and that's one of the Bible's most important themes.

THE VIOLENT PARTS

The second area where your congregation may struggle will be in the parts that are violent. I spent the year 2019 doing the reading plan myself in order to be better prepared to lead the congregation in 2020. I did the plan with a group of preacher friends who are part of my clergy covenant group. We found ourselves reading Kings and Chronicles during the time when the television series *Game of Thrones* was coming to an end. At one point, one of my clergy friends told us, "Today's reading makes an episode of *Game of Thrones* look like an episode of *Barney & Friends* or *Teletubbies*."

Here are some principles that you may want to consider and revisit often with the congregation, in order to help them through the violent parts of the Bible, especially in the light of Jesus and his commandment to love our enemies:

+ In ancient Israel and its surrounding cultures, obedience to God often involved violence, including fighting and killing enemies in the name of God. The emphasis in these texts is always on total devotion to God.
+ Jesus's teaching and death on the cross exposed the sin of violence and introduced new ways for us to be obedient today.
+ How can we be just as obedient as the ancient Israelites, except using the ways of obedience that God has given us today?

No, God will not call us to demonstrate obedience by slaughtering hundreds of false prophets, like Elijah was called to do in 1 Kings. But God does call us to obedience using the means that Jesus has shown us. Will we be just as faithful?

As our congregation read through Exodus, I devoted part of one of my sermons to the kind of wrestling we might do when we read the strong punishment language that God used in calling the Israelites to obey the commandments. Specifically, I unpacked Exodus 21, which occurs right after the famous Ten Commandments in Exodus 20. For obvious reasons, we choose to memorize those ten commandments, but we aren't really interested in committing the next chapter to memory:

+ In verse 21:2, "When you buy a male Hebrew slave, he will serve you for six years." (Wait, what?)
+ In verse 7: "When a man sells his daughter as a slave..." (Okay, stop right there. I don't even want to hear the rest.)

- Verse 15: "Anyone who violently kills their father or mother should be put to death." (Why do you have to say "violently" in that sentence?)

And it goes on. Kidnap a person, you're put to death. Curse your parents, you're put to death. Punch a pregnant woman and cause a miscarriage, you pay a fine. (Go figure.)

Earlier that week in our podcast episode, we interviewed Dr. Bo Adams of Candler School of Theology, and he suggested that Scriptures like these are like "wake up alarms" that remind us that the world of the Hebrew Bible is a very different culture from a very different era. So, one of our tasks as interpreters is to take truth that was meaningful in the text for that culture and translate into truth for ours.

One way to do that is to not see this as a "prescriptive" text—that is, one that prescribes how we *should* behave—but as a "descriptive" text—one that shows us the human condition and how we often *do* behave (whether we should or not), offering us a window into both ancient Israelite culture and our own. In other words, Exodus 21 doesn't tell us that we should own slaves, but rather that the ancient Israelites practiced slavery and that God cared about this detail of their lives as much as all the rest. These texts remind us that when left to our own devices, without "guardrails" as Bo Adams called it in the podcast, our default mode is to charm ourselves and each other.

But since our culture has changed, we don't need the same guardrails today that were necessary three thousand years ago. Slavery is no longer an accepted practice in most parts of the world (thank goodness). It is no longer necessary to have punishment that is an "eye for an eye" (thank goodness). We don't need to meet violence with violence (thank goodness).

So, even though the strong punishment language in Exodus is what worked as a guardrail for people three thousand years ago, we can (and should!) look for the kinds of guardrails that would guide and direct us in our culture today. Because our human condition hasn't changed, we need the guardrails that are adaptive to our times. That's the truth of Scripture. It's a way to take the Bible seriously, but not always literally.

THE UNSETTLING PARTS

Here is the other continuous pothole that congregations are sure to run into throughout the year. What do we do about the passages in the Bible where God does things that don't mesh with our understanding of God?

What about when God wants to destroy the world with a flood?

What about when God wants to do a sneak attack on Moses and kill him, right after God calls him?

What about when God demands Abraham to sacrifice his son Isaac?

What about when God orders the killing of people?

What about when God issues orders that not only make no sense to us, but paint a picture of God that we don't want anything to do with?

You are sure to get these questions—and to ask them yourself.

This is another theme that you will want to reinforce often throughout the year. We need to remember that the story of human civilization is tens of thousands of years old. The stories of the Bible involve humans that were here more than three thousand years ago.

Now, throughout history, this principle is still the same: God wants to be known by humans. God wants to be in a relationship with us. What that means is that God will use the language, imagery, and worldview that resonates with human beings at that particular time in order to connect with them.

The ancient worldview understood gods to act capriciously, which means free to act in a surprising way, with sudden shifts of mood and action. That was the language and the worldview at the time. So, God was revealed to them in those ways.

So, as humans have changed in their consciousness over time, that means that our views of God are also allowed to change over time. It is not that God changes. God always wants to be known by us and be in a relationship with us. What changes is the way we view God. And that change is not only permissible, it is natural.

Think about any relationship you have had with a person for a long period of time. Perhaps a spouse or a partner. Think about how your relationship with that person now is different from the way it was at the very beginning. Particularly in a courtship situation. At the beginning, you viewed that person in ways that were meaningful to you at the time. The thrill of dating, the anxiety of maybe breaking up, the questions of whether or not this person was "the one."

Now, years later, you see each other in different ways. Maybe more mature, nuanced ways that use a different love language or imagery that is more fitting for where your relationship is. Did either of you change? Perhaps in some ways, but you are still both essentially who you have always been. But has your relationship changed? Has the way you relate to each other changed? Absolutely.

The Old Testament records the ways humans related to God at the early stages of our courtship. We used language and imagery that were meaningful to us at the time, but now we see God differently because our relationship with God is allowed to change over time.

So, when we see troubling passages about God, it is permissible for us to say: "We don't see God in that way anymore. And that's both permissible and natural. It's important to understand our origins as human beings. So how do we view God now? Especially in light of Jesus and in light of our worldview today?"

This is a really important point, which you will want to reiterate often throughout the year. It will also be an opportunity for you to reinforce the need for people to read the Bible together, in a small group, and as part of this corporate journey.

Otherwise, reading the Old Testament by yourself and not having these kinds of insights along the way can lead a person toward atheism and agnosticism. People have said, "If this kind of God is at the center of the Judeo-Christian faith, then I want nothing to do with it."

Instead, we want to say, "This is evidence of how God wants to be known by us so much that God will relate to us in terms that we can understand at the time. So, the way we viewed God back then does not have to be the way we view God today."

CHAPTER 6

Pastoral Leadership
Expect, Embrace, Anticipate

As you prepare for this journey with your congregation, you may be experiencing a mixture of thoughts and emotions. With the anticipation there may be apprehension, as you wonder what might happen along the way.

What you can believe is that God *will* work. God promised the Israelites that when God speaks, the "word that comes from my mouth; / it does not return to me empty. / Instead, it does what I want, / and accomplishes what I intend" (Isaiah 55:11). You will experience that promise fulfilled, time and again, over the upcoming year.

You might also feel anxious about how you will keep up your own inner strength and spiritual stamina throughout this year. You may be worrying about burning out as you are preaching through the Bible. These are understandable feelings.

So, in this last chapter of this pastor guide, I want to offer you a few words of encouragement from our church's experience and some insights for you to remember as the pastoral leader of the church.

EXPECT SERENDIPITY

You will be amazed at the number of times you will begin preparing for a sermon with the thought, "Wow. This reading in the Bible has come

49

to us at just the right time." You may not see such possibilities now, as the prospect of leading your congregation may seem daunting. But God will use this journey to lead you and your people, just as God led the people of Israel throughout the Scriptures.

Your task will be a privileged one: to be the interpretive conduit through which your people can make connections between the Bible and their life together as a church.

Here are just a few examples of such "aha" moments for me, as we did the journey in 2020:

When the pandemic started and we first decided on Sunday, March 15, 2020, to suspend indoor worship, our text for the morning was the cry of the Israelites for a king. Their desire for comfort and protection from forces beyond their control resonated with exactly how we were feeling. I saw aspects of the anointing of Saul that I had never seen, and it helped us examine where we would place our trust in the midst of uncertainty.

A few weeks later, we read the stories of the divided kingdom of Israel, the dispersion of the Northern Kingdom by the Assyrians and the conquest of the Southern Kingdom by Babylon. We located ourselves in the experience of exile, far removed from comforting routines and rhythms, and longing for home.

Over the summer we experienced a nationwide reckoning over racial injustice in the wake of George Floyd's death. We also saw the death of civil rights icons John Lewis and C. T. Vivian. It was then that we read the stirring challenges of prophets like Isaiah and Jeremiah, who called us to recognize and oppose the injustices and inequalities of our day. We also drew lessons from the prophets about how to faithfully speak into political and social issues without aligning ourselves with partisan politics.

When our congregation was deliberating how to resume on-site worship and determined that we should create an outdoor worship area under a large tent on campus, we were reading and remembering prophetic words about both the Exodus and the Exile. We drew confidence in the stories of how we could worship God in a portable "tabernacle," wherever we were.

In the fall, when we were carefully considering how to have a stewardship campaign in a time of economic uncertainty and when people's personal finances were so fragile, we were reading Paul's letters to the churches. We claimed his gratitude for the church's generosity, as an encouragement for us to step into the story of God's ongoing work through the church.

Throughout your congregation's journey through the Bible, you will discover similar serendipitous moments, when the truths and insights of the Scriptures intersect with the needs of the moment in a remarkably timely fashion.

EMBRACE MYSTERY

It is inevitable that along the way, parishioners will come to you with deep, provocative questions about God and the Christian faith rooted in their reading of Scripture. It is also quite possible that many of these questions will be difficult for you to answer with a high degree of certainty.

As we read through the Bible at Hyde Park UMC, one congregation member in particular began taking note of various Scriptures that suggested what life would be like after we die. She astutely noticed that the Bible contains numerous descriptions, images, and metaphors to explain life after death, many of which appear to contradict each other. She noted the Hebrew concept of *sheol*, the promise of Jesus to the criminal that he would imminently join him in paradise, Paul's description in Thessalonians of the "dead in Christ" rising upon his return, and his metaphor of a seed to the Corinthians.

She asked me what we might conclude about these various perspectives and the uneasy conflict among them. How do we reconcile the Bible's differing voices, and how can we know for sure what happens after we die?

In moments like these, when you hear questions from parishioners about what they are reading and processing, take a moment to give thanks. You are experiencing the power of the Holy Spirit at work in your congregation, enabling them to employ their faculties of reason, tradition, and experience to encounter the authority of Scripture.

You are in a privileged position to serve as a docent in a gallery of faith, walking alongside your parishioners to point out aspects of these texts that they may not have noticed before, draw their attention to the beauty and power of the Scriptures, and prompt them to praise the Artist behind the artistry of the Scriptures.

It is in that context that you can also help your congregation embrace the mysteries of the Christian faith and the complexities of the Bible. It is likely that you have had to say to your parishioners the words "I don't know." Those words are honest and important. They not only remind us that we are limited in our ability to understand; they remind us that God is greater than our understanding. These questions can be evidence of God's infinite wisdom and power, beyond our ability to comprehend it, which can then be a source of comfort and solace to us. As writer Anne Lamott has said, "The opposite of faith is not doubt, but certainty." (*Plan B*; Riverhead Books, 2006; 256-257).

In other words, helping your congregation embrace the mystery of the faith, and find beauty in the complexities of the Scriptures, can be an enduring lesson in how to read the Bible without fear or frustration.

ANTICIPATE AMAZING

Finally, pay attention to the amazing work that God will do in your people as you take this journey together. They will discover insights into the texts and practical ways to apply them. They will deepen their relationships with others in the congregation and kindle new awareness of their capacities to serve, give, and love. They will develop new "muscle memory" for reading the Scriptures every day, which will endure after the year is over. And most of all, they will see their story in the stories of the Bible and experience the Holy Spirit working in them.

Here are just a few samples of what people at Hyde Park said after our year was over:

We made it. I am so proud of our group that we persevered during a very difficult time for many and for the world in which we live. Thanks to all of you for getting me through 2020 and the Bible. What an accomplishment!!

I knew Bible stories and a few Scripture passages. But reading it start to finish gave me a bigger picture and taught me things I didn't know. And it brought to life the stories I did know with new perspective. It gave me a greater appreciation of how God works in the world.

I have read and studied the Bible since I was a very young girl: Sunday school, Bible school, church camp, specialized Bible studies as a teenager. However, I had never read the Bible cover to cover until this year. Last fall, when I started hearing about The Bible 2020 project I was so excited that the opportunity was coming. I was geared up and ready on January 1, 2020! All of the resources along the way were so helpful and I used and appreciated all of them. Thank you to the entire church staff for putting this together for me, for our entire congregation.

It has finally helped to cement a picture for me as to the importance of knowing the Old as well as the New Testament. I truly had never read the entire Bible, and I am not sure I would ever have done so had it not been for the commitment our group made at the beginning of the year. As a leader who felt totally ill-equipped to be one, I delved deeper than I would have in order to share some insights with my group. Because of that, I have begun (I say that because there is never an end to reading the Bible!) to dig so much deeper when opening the Book, understanding that there are many interpretations to Scripture, and it is through the Spirit within me that I will learn my truths. I will forever be grateful to this church for having spearheaded this challenge.

I enjoyed the Old Testament much more than I imagined possible. I learned the Bible is more than a collection of stories and letters; it is one story with a beginning, middle, and end.

Blessings to you and your congregation as you go on this journey together!

APPENDIX

2020 Daily Reading and Sunday Schedule

Below is the full worship plan that we followed at Hyde Park UMC, integrating the daily reading plan with Sunday worship and the liturgical seasons during 2020. It contains the working titles of our thirteen worship series, the Scripture text used for Sunday worship, and the main key word that encapsulated the theme of the worship service for planning purposes.

As mentioned in Chapter 4, the first week's readings contain only four days. This gives you flexibility as your congregation begins the program, since January 1 is not the same weekday from one year to the next (and some may wish to start it at a different time of the year). For instance, in 2022, January 1 is a Saturday. You might use Sunday, January 2, to introduce the whole program, invite everyone to begin reading (Day 1) on Wednesday, January 5, and begin the first sermon series on January 9.

Season	Series Title	Day	Date	Daily Reading	Sunday Scripture & Key Word
Epiphany	The Story Begins	1	Jan. 1	Genesis 1:1–3:24	
		2	Jan. 2	Genesis 4:1–5:32	
		3	Jan. 3	Genesis 6:1–9:17	
		4	Jan. 4	Genesis 9:18–11:32	
		5	Jan. 5	Genesis 12:1–14:24	Genesis 1–2 Creation
		6	Jan. 6	Genesis 15:1–17:27	
		7	Jan. 7	Genesis 18:1–20:18	
		8	Jan. 8	Genesis 21:1–23:20	
		9	Jan. 9	Genesis 24:1–25:18	

Appendix

Season	Series Title	Day	Date	Daily Reading	Sunday Scripture & Key Word
Epiphany		10	Jan. 10	Genesis 25:19–28:9	
		11	Jan. 11	Genesis 28:10–30:43	
		12	Jan. 12	Genesis 31:1–36:43	Genesis 32:22-32 Family
		13	Jan. 13	Genesis 37:1–41:57	
		14	Jan. 14	Genesis 42:1–45:28	
		15	Jan. 15	Genesis 46:1–50:26	
		16	Jan. 16	Exodus 1:1–4:31	
		17	Jan. 17	Exodus 5:1–7:13	
		18	Jan. 18	Exodus 7:14–12:30	
		19	Jan. 19	Exodus 12:31–15:21	Exodus 14:1-30 Liberation
		20	Jan. 20	Exodus 15:22–18:27	
		21	Jan. 21	Exodus 19:1–21:36	
		22	Jan. 22	Exodus 22:1–24:18	
		23	Jan. 23	Exodus 25:1–27:21	
		24	Jan. 24	Exodus 28:1–30:38	
		25	Jan. 25	Exodus 31:1–34:35	
		26	Jan. 26	Exodus 35:1–40:38	Exodus 20:1-21 Community
		27	Jan. 27	Leviticus 1:1–4:35	

Season	Series Title	Day	Date	Daily Reading	Sunday Scripture & Key Word
Epiphany		28	Jan. 28	Leviticus 5:1–7:38	
		29	Jan. 29	Leviticus 8:1–10:20	
		30	Jan. 30	Leviticus 11:1–14:57	
		31	Jan. 31	Leviticus 15:1–18:30	
		32	Feb. 1	Leviticus 19:1–23:44	
	Road Rules	33	Feb. 2	Leviticus 24:1–27:34	Leviticus 16:1-22 Sacrifice
		34	Feb. 3	Numbers 1:1–4:49	
		35	Feb. 4	Numbers 5:1–7:89	
		36	Feb. 5	Numbers 8:1–10:36	
		37	Feb. 6	Numbers 11:1–14:45	
		38	Feb. 7	Numbers 15:1–18:32	
		39	Feb. 8	Numbers 19:1–21:35	
		40	Feb. 9	Numbers 22:1–25:18	Numbers 13:1-33 Faith
		41	Feb. 10	Numbers 26:1–31:54	
		42	Feb. 11	Numbers 32:1–36:13	
		43	Feb. 12	Deuteronomy 1:1–4:49	
		44	Feb. 13	Deuteronomy 5:1–8:20	
		45	Feb. 14	Deuteronomy 9:1–12:32	

Season	Series Title	Day	Date	Daily Reading	Sunday Scripture & Key Word
Epiphany		46	Feb. 15	Deuteronomy 13:1–16:22	
		47	Feb. 16	Deuteronomy 17:1–20:20	Deuteronomy 10:12-22 Commitment
		48	Feb. 17	Deuteronomy 21:1–25:19	
		49	Feb. 18	Deuteronomy 26:1–30:20	
		50	Feb. 19	Deuteronomy 31:1–34:12	
		51	Feb. 20	Joshua 1:1–3:17	
		52	Feb. 21	Joshua 4:1–6:27	
		53	Feb. 22	Joshua 7:1–11:23	
		54	Feb. 23	Joshua 12:1-17:18	Joshua 1:1-9 Courage
		55	Feb. 24	Joshua 18:1–24:33	
		56	Feb. 25	Judges 1:1–3:6	
Ash Wednesday	The Cross-Shaped Life	57	Feb. 26	Judges 3:7–5:31	Judges 7:1-8 Repentance
Lent		58	Feb. 27	Judges 6:1–8:35	
		59	Feb. 28	Judges 9:1–12:15	
		60	Feb. 29	Judges 13:1–16:31	
Lent 1	Holy Character From	61	Mar. 1	Judges 17:1–21:25	Ruth 1:6-22 Loyalty
	Royal Heroes	62	Mar. 2	Ruth 1:1–2:23	
		63	Mar. 3	Ruth 3:1–4:22	

Season	Series Title	Day	Date	Daily Reading	Sunday Scripture & Key Word
Lent 1		64	Mar. 4	1 Samuel 1:1–3:21	
		65	Mar. 5	1 Samuel 4:1–7:17	
		66	Mar. 6	1 Samuel 8:1–12:25	
		67	Mar. 7	1 Samuel 13:1–15:35	
Lent 2		68	Mar. 8	1 Samuel 16:1–17:58	1 Samuel 3:1-21 Attentiveness
		69	Mar. 9	1 Samuel 18:1–20:42	
		70	Mar. 10	1 Samuel 21:1–24:22	
		71	Mar. 11	1 Samuel 25:1–28:25	
		72	Mar. 12	1 Samuel 29:1–31:13	
		73	Mar. 13	2 Samuel 1:1–4:12	
		74	Mar. 14	2 Samuel 5:1–7:29	
Lent 3		75	Mar. 15	2 Samuel 8:1–10:19	1 Samuel 16:1-13 Character
		76	Mar. 16	2 Samuel 11:1–14:33	
		77	Mar. 17	2 Samuel 15:1–19:43	
		78	Mar. 18	2 Samuel 20:1–24:25	
		79	Mar. 19	1 Kings 1:1–4:34	
		80	Mar. 20	1 Kings 5:1–8:66	
		81	Mar. 21	1 Kings 9:1–11:43	

Season	Series Title	Day	Date	Daily Reading	Sunday Scripture & Key Word
Lent 4		82	Mar. 22	1 Kings 12:1–16:34	1 Kings 3:1-15 Wisdom
		83	Mar. 23	1 Kings 17:1–19:21	
		84	Mar. 24	1 Kings 20:1–22:53	
		85	Mar. 25	2 Kings 1:1–8:15	
		86	Mar. 26	2 Kings 8:16–10:36	
		87	Mar. 27	2 Kings 11:1–13:25	
		88	Mar. 28	2 Kings 14:1–17:41	
Lent 5		89	Mar. 29	2 Kings 18:1–21:26	1 Kings 19:1-18 Hope
		90	Mar. 30	2 Kings 22:1–25:30	
		91	Mar. 31	1 Chronicles 1:1–9:44	
		92	Apr. 1	1 Chronicles 10:1–12:40	
		93	Apr. 2	1 Chronicles 13:1–16:43	
		94	Apr. 3	1 Chronicles 17:1–22:1	
		95	Apr. 4	1 Chronicles 22:2–27:34	
Lent 6		96	Apr. 5	1 Chronicles 28:1–29:30	2 Kings 23:1-14 Obedience
Holy Week	Holy Week	97	Apr. 6	2 Chronicles 1:1–5:1	
		98	Apr. 7	2 Chronicles 5:2–9:31	
		99	Apr. 8	2 Chronicles 10:1–13:22	

Season	Series Title	Day	Date	Daily Reading	Sunday Scripture & Key Word
Maundy Thursday		100	Apr. 9	2 Chronicles 14:1–16:14	
Good Friday		101	Apr. 10	2 Chronicles 17:1–20:37	
Holy Saturday		102	Apr. 11	2 Chronicles 21:1–24:27	
Easter Sunday	Easter	103	Apr. 12	2 Chronicles 25:1–28:27	Mark 16:1-8 Resurrection
Easter	A Spiritual Makeover	104	Apr. 13	2 Chronicles 29:1–32:33	
		105	Apr. 14	2 Chronicles 33:1–36:23	
	Easter As A Return From Exile	106	Apr. 15	Ezra 1:1–3:13	
		107	Apr. 16	Ezra 4:1–6:22	
		108	Apr. 17	Ezra 7:1–10:44	
		109	Apr. 18	Nehemiah 1:1–4:23	
		110	Apr. 19	Nehemiah 5:1–7:73	Nehemiah 8:1-12 Reform
		111	Apr. 20	Nehemiah 8:1–10:39	
		112	Apr. 21	Nehemiah 11:1–13:31	
		113	Apr. 22	Esther 1:1–4:17	
		114	Apr. 23	Esther 5:1–10:3	
		115	Apr. 24	Job 1:1–5:27	
		116	Apr. 25	Job 6:1–14:22	
		117	Apr. 26	Job 15:1–21:34	Esther 4:1-17 Courage

Season	Series Title	Day	Date	Daily Reading	Sunday Scripture & Key Word
Easter		118	Apr. 27	Job 22:1–31:40	
		119	Apr. 28	Job 32:1–37:24	
		120	Apr. 29	Job 38:1–42:17	
		121	Apr. 30	Psalms 1:1–4:8	
		122	May 1	Psalms 5:1–8:9	
		123	May 2	Psalms 9:1–12:8	
	God's Favorite Playlist	124	May 3	Psalms 13:1–16:11	Psalm 7 A Song of Help
		125	May 4	Psalms 17:1–20:9	
		126	May 5	Psalms 21:1–24:10	
		127	May 6	Psalms 25:1–28:9	
		128	May 7	Psalms 29:1–32:11	
		129	May 8	Psalms 33:1–36:12	
		130	May 9	Psalms 37:1–41:13	
		131	May 10	Psalms 42:1–45:17	Psalm 23 A Song of Comfort
		132	May 11	Psalms 46:1–49:20	
		133	May 12	Psalms 50:1–53:6	
		134	May 13	Psalms 54:1–56:13	
		135	May 14	Psalms 57:1–59:17	

Season	Series Title	Day	Date	Daily Reading	Sunday Scripture & Key Word
Easter		136	May 15	Psalms 60:1–63:11	
		137	May 16	Psalms 64:1–68:35	
		138	May 17	Psalms 69:1–72:20	Psalm 51 A Song of Confession
		139	May 18	Psalms 73:1–75:10	
		140	May 19	Psalms 76:1–78:72	
		141	May 20	Psalms 79:1–84:12	
		142	May 21	Psalms 85:1–89:52	
		143	May 22	Psalms 90:1–95:11	
		144	May 23	Psalms 96:1–101:8	
		145	May 24	Psalms 102:1–104:35	Psalm 100 A Song of Praise
		146	May 25	Psalms 105:1–107:43	
		147	May 26	Psalms 108:1–112:10	
		148	May 27	Psalms 113:1–118:29	
		149	May 28	Psalm 119:1-88	
		150	May 29	Psalm 119:89-176	
		151	May 30	Psalms 120:1-126:6	
Pentecost Sunday		152	May 31	Psalms 127:1–130:8	Psalm 150; Acts 2:1-12 A Song of Celebration
Ordinary Time		153	June 1	Psalms 131:1–136:26	

Season	Series Title	Day	Date	Daily Reading	Sunday Scripture & Key Word
Ordinary Time		154	June 2	Psalms 137:1–140:13	
		155	June 3	Psalms 141:1–144:15	
		156	June 4	Psalms 145:1–150:6	
		157	June 5	Proverbs 1:1–2:22	
		158	June 6	Proverbs 3:1-35	
	The Wise Life	159	June 7	Proverbs 4:1–5:23	Proverbs 3:1-12 Trust
		160	June 8	Proverbs 6:1–7:27	
		161	June 9	Proverbs 8:1–9:18	
		162	June 10	Proverbs 10:1–11:31	
		163	June 11	Proverbs 12:1–13:25	
		164	June 12	Proverbs 14:1-35	
		165	June 13	Proverbs 15:1-33	
		166	June 14	Proverbs 16:1-33	Proverbs 12:13-28 Holiness
		167	June 15	Proverbs 17:1–18:24	
		168	June 16	Proverbs 19:1–20:30	
		169	June 17	Proverbs 21:1–22:29	
		170	June 18	Proverbs 23:1-35	
		171	June 19	Proverbs 24:1-34	

SEASON	SERIES TITLE	DAY	DATE	DAILY READING	SUNDAY SCRIPTURE & KEY WORD
Ordinary Time		172	June 20	Proverbs 25:1–26:28	
		173	June 21	Proverbs 27:1–29:27	Proverbs 16:1-20 Integrity
		174	June 22	Proverbs 30:1-33	
		175	June 23	Proverbs 31:1-31	
		176	June 24	Ecclesiastes 1:1–2:26	
		177	June 25	Ecclesiates 3:1–5:20	
		178	June 26	Ecclesiates 6:1–8:17	
		179	June 27	Ecclesiates 9:1–12:14	
		180	June 28	Song of Solomon 1:1–4:16	Ecclesiastes 3:1-15 Time
		181	June 29	Song of Solomon 5:1–8:14	
		182	June 30	Isaiah 1:1–4:6	
		183	July 1	Isaiah 5:1–7:25	
		184	July 2	Isaiah 8:1–11:16	
		185	July 3	Isaiah 12:1–16:14	
		186	July 4	Isaiah 17:1–23:18	
	Hope For Hard Times	187	July 5	Isaiah 24:1–27:13	Isaiah 6:1-13 Consecration
		188	July 6	Isaiah 28:1–31:9	
		189	July 7	Isaiah 32:1–35:10	

Season	Series Title	Day	Date	Daily Reading	Sunday Scripture & Key Word
Ordinary Time		190	July 8	Isaiah 36:1–39:8	
		191	July 9	Isaiah 40:1–44:28	
		192	July 10	Isaiah 45:1–48:22	
		193	July 11	Isaiah 49:1–52:12	
		194	July 12	Isaiah 52:13–55:13	Isaiah 43:1-7 Restoration
		195	July 13	Isaiah 56:1–59:21	
		196	July 14	Isaiah 60:1–66:24	
		197	July 15	Jeremiah 1:1–4:31	
		198	July 16	Jeremiah 5:1–8:17	
		199	July 17	Jeremiah 8:18–12:17	
		200	July 18	Jeremiah 13:1–16:21	
		201	July 19	Jeremiah 17:1–20:18	Jeremiah 1:4-10; 3:6-14 Courage
		202	July 20	Jeremiah 21:1–24:10	
		203	July 21	Jeremiah 25:1–29:32	
		204	July 22	Jeremiah 30:1–33:26	
		205	July 23	Jeremiah 34:1–38:28	
		206	July 24	Jeremiah 39:1–45:5	
		207	July 25	Jeremiah 46:1–49:39	

Appendix

Season	Series Title	Day	Date	Daily Reading	Sunday Scripture & Key Word
Ordinary Time		208	July 26	Jeremiah 50:1–52:34	Jeremiah 31:31-40 Covenant
		209	July 27	Lamentations 1:1–2:22	
		210	July 28	Lamentations 3:1–5:22	
		211	July 29	Ezekiel 1:1–5:17	
		212	July 30	Ezekiel 6:1–11:25	
		213	July 31	Ezekiel 12:1–16:63	
		214	Aug. 1	Ezekiel 17:1–21:32	
	Faith When It Counts	215	Aug. 2	Ezekiel 22:1–26:21	Ezekiel 1:15-28 Vision
		216	Aug. 3	Ezekiel 27:1–32:32	
		217	Aug. 4	Ezekiel 33:1–37:28	
		218	Aug. 5	Ezekiel 38:1–42:20	
		219	Aug. 6	Ezekiel 43:1–48:35	
		220	Aug. 7	Daniel 1:1–3:30	
		221	Aug. 8	Daniel 4:1–6:28	
		222	Aug. 9	Daniel 7:1–12:13	Daniel 6:10-28 Faithfulness
		223	Aug. 10	Hosea 1:1–5:15	
		224	Aug. 11	Hosea 6:1–10:15	
		225	Aug. 12	Hosea 11:1–14:9	

Season	Series Title	Day	Date	Daily Reading	Sunday Scripture & Key Word
Ordinary Time		226	Aug. 13	Joel 1:1–3:21	
		227	Aug. 14	Amos 1:1–4:13	
		228	Aug. 15	Amos 5:1–9:15	
		229	Aug.16	Obadiah 1-21	Jonah 1:1-17 Reluctance
		230	Aug. 17	Jonah 1:1–2:10	
		231	Aug. 18	Jonah 3:1–4:11	
		232	Aug. 19	Micah 1:1–4:13	
		233	Aug. 20	Micah 5:1–7:20	
		234	Aug. 21	Nahum 1:1–3:19	
		235	Aug. 22	Habakkuk 1:1–3:19	
		236	Aug. 23	Zephaniah 1:1–3:20	Micah 6:8 Justice
		237	Aug. 24	Haggai 1:1–2:23	
		238	Aug. 25	Zechariah 1:1–4:14	
		239	Aug. 26	Zechariah 5:1–9:17	
		240	Aug. 27	Zechariah 10:1–14:21	
		241	Aug. 28	Malachi 1:1–2:17	
		242	Aug. 29	Malachi 3:1–4:6	
	The Jesus Story	243	Aug. 30	Matthew 1:1–2:23	Matthew 5:17-48 Law

Season	Series Title	Day	Date	Daily Reading	Sunday Scripture & Key Word
Ordinary Time		244	Aug. 31	Matthew 3:1–4:25	
		245	Sep. 1	Matthew 5:1-48	
		246	Sep. 2	Matthew 6:1-34	
		247	Sep. 3	Matthew 7:1–8:34	
		248	Sep. 4	Matthew 9:1–10:42	
		249	Sep. 5	Matthew 11:1–12:50	
		250	Sep. 6	Matthew 13:1-58	Matthew 23:1-36 Hypocrisy
		251	Sep. 7	Matthew 14:1–15:39	
		252	Sep. 8	Matthew 16:1–18:35	
		253	Sep. 9	Matthew 19:1–20:34	
		254	Sep. 10	Matthew 21:1-46	
		255	Sep. 11	Matthew 22:1–23:39	
		256	Sep. 12	Matthew 24:1–25:46	
		257	Sep. 13	Matthew 26:1-75	Mark 1:16-20 Follow
		258	Sep. 14	Matthew 27:1–28:20	
		259	Sep. 15	Mark 1:1–3:35	
		260	Sep. 16	Mark 4:1–5:43	
		261	Sep. 17	Mark 6:1-56	

Season	Series Title	Day	Date	Daily Reading	Sunday Scripture & Key Word
Ordinary Time		262	Sep. 18	Mark 7:1–8:38	
		263	Sep. 19	Mark 9:1–10:45	
		264	Sep. 20	Mark 10:46–12:34	Mark 9:14-29 Belief
		265	Sep. 21	Mark 12:35–13:37	
		266	Sep. 22	Mark 14:1-72	
		267	Sep. 23	Mark 15:1–16:20	
		268	Sep. 24	Luke 1:1-80	
		269	Sep. 25	Luke 2:1-52	
		270	Sep. 26	Luke 3:1–4:13	
		271	Sep. 27	Luke 4:14–5:39	Luke 4:14-30 Good News
		272	Sep. 28	Luke 6:1-49	
		273	Sep. 29	Luke 7:1–8:39	
		274	Sep. 30	Luke 8:40–9:62	
		275	Oct. 1	Luke 10:1–11:36	
		276	Oct. 2	Luke 11:37–12:59	
		277	Oct. 3	Luke 13:1–14:35	
		278	Oct. 4	Luke 15:1–16:31	Luke 15:1-32 Found
		279	Oct. 5	Luke 17:1–18:43	

Season	Series Title	Day	Date	Daily Reading	Sunday Scripture & Key Word
Ordinary Time		280	Oct. 6	Luke 19:1-48	
		281	Oct. 7	Luke 20:1–21:38	
		282	Oct. 8	Luke 22:1-71	
		283	Oct. 9	Luke 23:1-56	
		284	Oct. 10	Luke 24:1-53	
		285	Oct. 11	John 1:1–2:12	John 1:1-18 Logos
		286	Oct. 12	John 2:13–3:36	
		287	Oct. 13	John 4:1-54	
		288	Oct. 14	John 5:1–6:21	
		289	Oct. 15	John 6:22–7:9	
		290	Oct. 16	John 7:10–8:59	
		291	Oct. 17	John 9:1–10:42	
		292	Oct. 18	John 11:1–12:50	John 15:1-17 Jesus
		293	Oct. 19	John 13:1–14:31	
		294	Oct. 20	John 15:1–17:26	
		295	Oct. 21	John 18:1–19:42	
		296	Oct. 22	John 20:1–21:25	
		297	Oct. 23	Acts 1:1–2:47	

Season	Series Title	Day	Date	Daily Reading	Sunday Scripture & Key Word
Ordinary Time		298	Oct. 24	Acts 3:1–5:16	
	Ancestry: Our Spiritual DNA	299	Oct. 25	Acts 5:17–7:60	Acts 2:41-47 Church
		300	Oct. 26	Acts 8:1–9:43	
		301	Oct. 27	Acts 10:1–12:25	
		302	Oct. 28	Acts 13:1–15:21	
		303	Oct. 29	Acts 15:22–17:34	
		304	Oct. 30	Acts 18:1–20:38	
		305	Oct. 31	Acts 21:1–23:35	
All Saints' Sunday		306	Nov. 1	Acts 24:1–26:32	Acts 15:1-29 Inclusion
Ordinary Time		307	Nov. 2	Acts 27:1–28:31	
		308	Nov. 3	Romans 1:1–3:20	
		309	Nov. 4	Romans 3:21–5:21	
		310	Nov. 5	Romans 6:1–8:17	
		311	Nov. 6	Romans 8:18–10:21	
		312	Nov. 7	Romans 11:1–13:14	
	Step Into This Story	313	Nov. 8	Romans 14:1–16:27	Romans 12:1-21 Impact
	(Stewardship Emphasis)	314	Nov. 9	1 Corinthians 1:1–3:23	

Season	Series Title	Day	Date	Daily Reading	Sunday Scripture & Key Word
Ordinary Time		315	Nov. 10	1 Corinthians 4:1–6:20	
		316	Nov. 11	1 Corinthians 7:1–9:27	
		317	Nov. 12	1 Corinthians 10:1–12:31	
		318	Nov. 13	1 Corinthians 13:1–16:24	
		319	Nov. 14	2 Corinthians 1:1–3:18	
		320	Nov. 15	2 Corinthians 4:1–7:16	2 Corinthians 8:1-7 Generosity
		321	Nov. 16	2 Corinthians 8:1–10:18	
		322	Nov. 17	2 Corinthians 11:1–13:13	
		323	Nov. 18	Galatians 1:1–2:21	
		324	Nov. 19	Galatians 3:1–4:31	
		325	Nov. 20	Galatians 5:1–6:18	
		326	Nov. 21	Ephesians 1:1–2:22	
		327	Nov. 22	Ephesians 3:1–4:32	Ephesians 4:1-16 Unity
		328	Nov. 23	Ephesians 5:1–6:24	
		329	Nov. 24	Philippians 1:1–2:30	
		330	Nov. 25	Philippians 3:1–4:23	
		331	Nov. 26	Colossians 1:1–2:23	

Season	Series Title	Day	Date	Daily Reading	Sunday Scripture & Key Word
Ordinary Time		332	Nov. 27	Colossians 3:1–4:18	
		333	Nov. 28	1 Thessalonians 1:1–3:13	
Advent 1	The Good Life	334	Nov. 29	1 Thessalonians 4:1–5:28	1 Thessalonians 5:16-24 Hope
		335	Nov. 30	2 Thessalonians 1:–3:18	
		336	Dec. 1	1 Timothy 1:1–3:16	
		337	Dec. 2	1 Timothy 4:1–6:21	
		338	Dec. 3	2 Timothy 1:1–2:26	
		339	Dec. 4	2 Timothy 3:1–4:22	
		340	Dec. 5	Titus 1:1–3:15	
Advent 2		341	Dec. 6	Philemon 1-25	1 Timothy 2:1-2 Peace
		342	Dec. 7	Hebrews 1:1–3:19	
		343	Dec. 8	Hebrews 4:1–6:20	
		344	Dec. 9	Hebrews 7:1–9:28	
		345	Dec. 10	Hebrews 10:1–11:40	
		346	Dec. 11	Hebrews 12:1–13:25	
		347	Dec. 12	James 1:1–2:26	
Advent 3		348	Dec. 13	James 3:1–5:20	James 1:2-4 Joy
		349	Dec. 14	1 Peter 1:1–2:25	

Season	Series Title	Day	Date	Daily Reading	Sunday Scripture & Key Word
Advent 3		350	Dec. 15	1 Peter 3:1–5:14	
		351	Dec. 16	2 Peter 1:1–2:22	
		352	Dec. 17	2 Peter 3:1-18	
		353	Dec. 18	1 John 1:1–3:24	
		354	Dec. 19	1 John 4:1–5:21	
Advent 4		355	Dec. 20	2 John 1-12	1 John 3:11-24 Love
		356	Dec. 21	3 John 1-15	
		357	Dec. 22	Jude 1-25	
		358	Dec. 23	Revelation 1:1–2:29	
Christmas		359	Dec. 24	Revelation 3:1–5:14	Luke 2:1-20 Light
		360	Dec. 25	Revelation 6:1–8:5	
		361	Dec. 26	Revelation 8:6–11:19	
Christmas 1	Amen, Hallelujah	362	Dec. 27	Revelation 12:1–14:20	Revelation 21:1-6 Heaven
		363	Dec. 28	Revelation 15:1–17:18	
		364	Dec. 29	Revelation 18:1–20:15	
		365	Dec. 30	Revelation 21:1–22:21	
		366	Dec. 31	Amen	

Resources for Learning to Read
the Bible without Fear or Frustration

The following are resources that we often referred people to throughout the year:

Bibleproject2020.org. This is our church's website that contains all the material that we developed to guide the congregation in the journey. It includes links to our sermons, reading plan, devotionals, and podcast.

"The Bible 2020" Podcast. Available through Apple Podcasts, Spotify, Overcast, and many other podcast websites. This was a centerpiece to our journey. Each episode is less than twenty-five minutes and features an in-depth interview with a biblical scholar, clergy, or layperson who gives insights into the week's readings. Many small groups listened to these episodes as part of their weekly sessions.

Amplifymedia.com. This streaming service contains the weekly videos for small groups to use for The Bible Year, along with many other Bible studies and resources. Subscriptions are available for your whole congregation or for individuals.

Bibleproject.com. This website contains informative videos that offer helpful introductions to each biblical book, along with other insights into the Scriptures.

Making Sense of the Bible: Rediscovering the Power of Scripture Today by Adam Hamilton. A helpful book that guides people in faithfully interpreting the difficult parts of the Bible. Our youth program spent the year reading and studying this book.

Manna and Mercy: A Brief History of God's Unfolding Promise to Mend the Entire Universe (**mannaandmercy.org**) A beautiful and insightful 100-page graphic novel that depicts the stories of the Bible, uniting them with the overarching theme of God's love. It is both an accessible primer and a deep dive into the narratives of the Bible.

Resources for Youth, Children, and Adult Ministries

Our children and youth programs followed their own parallel track through the stories of the Bible, using curriculum produced by the following companies:

"The Story." Zondervan Publishing. Thirty-one lessons that capture the main stories and themes of the Bible.

"Digging into the Bible in One Year." Group Publishing. Fifty-two weekly lessons, divided into quarters, with lesson plans, videos, and other supplemental material.